INDIAN SUMMER

Poems
by
Agnes Yarnall

DORRANCE & COMPANY, INCORPORATED
828 LANCASTER AVENUE • BRYN MAWR, PENNSYLVANIA 19010
Publishers Since 1920

Copyright © 1985 by Agnes Yarnall
All Rights Reserved
ISBN 0-8059-3004-3
Printed in the United States of America
First Printing

To my father, Charlton Yarnall
and
to my sister, Anna-Sophia

Contents

Indian Summer	1
The Violet Snails	2
The Green Tree	3
Domino	4
Tonight	6
Wind From the West	7
Parent Mine!	9
"What Will You Do 'With These Things' When I Am Gone?"	10
To C.Y.	11
Everyday *After A Death*	12
Evening In the Hospital	13
The Robin	14
Nostalgia	15
Moonlight	16
Coronation	17
New Years '84–'85	18
The Rocking Horse	19
In the Days of My Youth—	20
Long Ago	21
The Photograph	22
The Winter of Discontent	23
Christmas—1962	24
No Chipmunk	25
The Last Trout	26
To A Friend Who Died Too Soon	27
Happening	28
The Seminoles	29
The Deer	31
Cape Horn	32
The Storm	33
The Kingdom of Heaven	34
The Caught Fish	36
The Lost Island	37

The Union Jack	38
Sonnet	39
Differences	40
La Strada	41
Sonnet to Keats	42
The Turtle	43
Night Club	45
Maine	46
Two Deer	47
Man	48
Achilles Heel	50
Concerto	51
Below Surface	52
Where?	53
A Voice Speaks In Hades	54
Landing	55
The House	56
Hurdy-Gurdy Monkey	58
Streetcorner	59
The Window *Saint Mary's by the Sea*	61
The Song	62
Ships	63
The Pine Tree	64
For Anna-Sophia:*How Brave You Were!*	65
The Orchard	66
To Anna-Sophia:*Do You Remember?*	67
Revolution	68
My Dog	69
The Christmas Tree	70

Indian Summer

The blue of the sea is in my eyes,
And the trees in their golden glory—
And the rocks of granite mounting high
Like a fort in a fairy story—

The waves, disturbed from a distant storm,
Crash, leaving wreaths of foam,
And all of nature combines to say
To the traveller, "Go not home!"

There will be no tumbling ocean,
There will be no wildness near,
I cannot look from my door yard
And see a startled deer—

My memory holds the beauty
Even if we must part,
But the blue of the sea remaineth
Awash in my restless heart!

The Violet Snails

The violet snails
Lie on the beach,
Blown there by the southeast wind—
O exquisite fragility of shell!
Like a horn, round and curved and delicate,
Thinner than paper,
Lighter than a leaf!
Violet snails
Riding, riding
In a sublimity of courage
Over the wild foaming mountains
Of the Gulf Stream!
Over the reef you came in the early morning,
An armada of tiny purple ships
Sliding down the tall green breakers,
Carried miraculously unbroken on the foam
To this quiet beach at last—
Here in the sun I found you,
O voyaging violet beauty
From the southern sea!

The Green Tree

The green tree of youth
  Holds the music of remembering
    In its leaves—
Every spring it returns
  Like the cardinal,
Or the mourning dove—
  Under the blowing pattern
    Of wind and sun
      It is there—
The moment locked in green!
  The drowning of the heart
    On a summer afternoon!
The leaves heavy in the heat
  And the birds singing—
    The moment—gone!
But always forever there!

Domino

I am a clown
Going down, for the last time
Into a sea of mirth—
Soon it will be over,
And I, like a discarded lover,
Will no longer have to dance—
I will no longer see
The tent top over me—
The noise of the circus,
The glittering bells and jingles,
Will be over—
There will be no more paint
And I will not have to faint
Of my broken heart,
In order to amuse the kings and queens.
I will no longer leap
Through hoops—and weep
For my departed love,
Oh God above,
She was untrue anyway!
I shall no longer smell
The sawdust in this gaudy hell—
For there is something whispers,
"You are dying,
And all through with lying—
Now the blaze of light
Will dazzle you no longer,
For the last goodnight
Is hovering near your heart—
Another start
Awaits you in the grave—
And you will have
Only the lonely stars and sleep!
You will not need to weep

Once more, O clown,
Clown with the painted face,
Clown who is going down
Into the earth's embrace!

Tonight

The stars so bright tonight,
The moon so clear!
The night so beautiful,
The stars so near!
England itself might seem
As near or far
As that clear moon, or that
Adjacent star—
If thoughts are winged, then
Proximity
Is mine for thinking thus,
Immediately:
And like the travelling moon,
And like the star—
In this sweet moment
I am where you are!

Wind From the West

Across the state of California
Came the wind!
Over the green valleys it came,
Over the vineyards
Sweeping up into itself
The sweetness of the new grapes
Hot in the sun;
On it came, like a tide
Pouring over the Sierra Nevadas,
Taking some of the sharpness of the snow
Into its streaming force—
Over Utah it came,
Sucking into itself
The heavy bitterness of salt
From the white water of the lake—
Over Wyoming, over Nebraska
Flew the wind,
Absorbing the scent of pine
And of leather,
Of dusty sugar-beets,
And the iron winter-earth of the prairies!
On went the wind
Over the flat cornfields of Iowa
Into Illinois—
At the touch of the wind,
The immense surface of Lake Michigan
Broke into rough blue waves
Cream-crested and rolling
Onward, ever onward
Under the urging of the wind!
The skyscrapers in Chicago
Swayed slightly,
Their high windows singing
With the music of the wind—

On, on, it went
Over Indiana and Ohio,
Over Pittsburgh, city of smoke,
Pouring through the valleys of the Alleghenies,
An invisible river of sound and force—
The rolling farmlands of Pennsylvania
Stretched out beneath the wind,
As on and on it came—
Blowing ever eastward—
Sweeping past the glittering towers of New York,
Out over the Atlantic Ocean
Through the night, through the stars—
Taking with it my thoughts of you, my love!

Parent Mine

If I hear the ring of axe
   Cutting tree,
How it brings remembrance back,
   Back to me!
How I strain my eyes to see
   Who is there,
Is he tall and straight and slim,
   Brown of hair?
Blue of eye, and proud of nose,
   Parent mine!
Has he hands to chop a tree?
   Prune a vine?
Make a doll's house for a child,
   Mend a chair?
Fix a fire so the flame
   Sucks the air?
Has he tenderness like gold?
   Heart of fire,
Holds he all my loyal love?
   My undoubted sire!
Loves he creatures over-much,
   So to shun
Cruel trap and wily snare,
   Use of gun!
Has he humor, and a wit
   Sharp as knife?
Would he give to those he loves
   All his life?
See him standing, shirt of grey,
   By the fallen tree
Wood-smoke rising in the air—
   This my memory!

"What Will You Do With these Things When I Am Gone?"

Saint Cecilia on the wall,
   Portrait on the stair,
Fire burning, stool beside
   Pink familiar chair—
Black oak table, double lamp
   Bronze mermen to hold,
All the things you had about
   As you were growing old—
Now surrounding us, they stand—
   Here and here and here
Fell your hand, or lay your book,
   These things to endear—
Loved I them before this time,
   Now how greatly more!
Since they speak to me of you
   Who have gone before—

To C.Y.

The little Christmas tree is still
   Beneath its weight of stars
And carols echo through the air
   In frosty avatars.

The fire glances ruby-red
   To warm the Christmas guest,
It cannot warm you any more
   Who lie in icy rest.

Who lie away from me tonight
   My Parent through the years—
I cannot see the fire now
   Because of these quick tears.

Yet as of old I hear your voice
   "Be strong, my child, be brave—"
Death has no sting for such as you
   Who help me from the grave.

Everyday
After A Death

Everyday is the surface of the sea—
   Everyday is the clear blue,
   Or the clear green,
   Jagged or calm,
   Still or cut by the wind—
This is everyday—this is nine o'clock,
     Or ten o'clock,
Or eight-in-the-morning, breakfast time—
   Any hour of the day, it might be,
   Even the evening,
As long as there are people about—
   But at night time—or the time later,
Or the time in the brain behind the eyes
That have closed for forty winks or more,
That time is the real time—
   It is the black abyss of thought,
   The moon of memory
   Rising in the recollection of the mind,
   The river of reminiscence
     Nearly fifty years long,
Rising, rising,
   Pouring its black tumult
Into the quiet harbor of my heart.

Evening In the Hospital

I do not remember very much,
But I remember this—
A circle of lamp light,
A bit of evening sky
Darkblue, cut in a triangle;
The light on your hair,
Your collar, sharp in its whiteness
Against your neck;
Your hands, more beautiful to me than any others,
Holding in their long fingers the yellow paper book.
The rest of the room dark
Outside the circle of light—
And the sound of your voice,
Slow, English, reminiscent
Of another country, another life,
Somehow mysteriously interwoven with mine!
So different, so alike!
Your voice reading, reading
The long evenings away while I was ill,
And the slow deep warm wave of your love
Flowing over my tormented spirit,
Bringing peace at last.

The Robin

Move thou thy head, O robin, once again!
Open thine eye that but a moment hence
Looked up and down the stretch of wide blue sky!
Lie not so warm and heavy in my hand,
Lie not so limp, O little shattered bird;
Lift but thy wing, O robin,
And all my leaden heart will lighter be,
To know thee still alive in spite of me!

On having unwittingly killed a robin
Which flew into my car.

Nostalgia

Only the yellow buttercups that fall
Petal by petal;
Only the song of the cardinal,
Falling note by liquid note,
Through the elm tree;
Only the sharp beauty of the Spring,
Falling, falling
Bitterly sweet
In a wave of pink and white;
Only the running stream
Falling like glass
Over the lichened stone;
Only the willow
Spraying its chute of tears
Upon the grass;
Only these things—
Not voices, not people,
Not city streets, nor lights,
Nor a romantic moment anywhere,
Can at all replace your loss,
Save these—
These, unlike people, do not speak of you,
But they recall
Your mood, the things you said of them,
Thus to my empty heart
They bring you near.

Moonlight

Across the narrow darkness
   The moonlight entered in—
It fell upon the carpet
   Like strips of silver tin—
It touched the edge of sofa
   And caught around a chair
And found the corner's blackness
   And penetrated there—
The corner melted backward
   And where there was dark before
A cool enameled silver
   Disturbed the secret floor

Coronation

O Pageantry of Pomp and Power,
O color rising wave on wave,
This is the England I remember
The glorious, the brave!

This is the breed that followed Nelson
Count their victories ten by ten,
Defeat is a word they do not reckon,
These are the Island men!

When the Armada came to England
Fought they under another Queen,
Bowled and smiled and saved Old England,
The rocky Island green!

Ye who are watching England's splendor
Marching by like a living flame,
Honour this nation now, forever,
Her's is a deathless name!

New Years '84–'85

Blessings have I abounding
   Here at home,
But none like this
   When good friends choose to come

Here to my hearthstone
   Welcoming the new,
And so I drink to you
   And you and you!

Witness the warmth!
   It rises in the air
Untinged by misery,
   Knowing not despair—

How can I tell you?
   How can I make it clear?
Your affection is my bulwark
   For the year!

The Rocking Horse

It stood—beautiful in its paint
  Black and white,
Fiery eyes, silver bridle,
  Ready to be ridden
Gently or wildly,
  Savagely or quietly
Over meadows and streams
  And through woods
Atremble with spring
  Or quiet with winter snow.
It was fed upon violets and sugar,
  Loved goldenrod
    And asters,
And once by the seashore
  Had gone wild with joy
    And drunk great gulps
Of the bitter salty sea!
  How dear was the rocking horse
  And how magical!
My uncle named it Hector,
  But that was not it at all—
Because once when I threw my
  Arms around its neck,
Loving it so dearly as a child will,
  It whispered to me in love
"Hector is not my name at all,
  I am called Pegasus!"

In the Days of My Youth—

In the days of my youth
The earth was rich,
The air elixir,
The sun a passionate blessing,
The starry night
Beautiful in extreme!
There were polished doorknobs,
Scrubbed steps,
The sound of rollerskates
Running over the uneven brick pavement,
And the knife grinder called his tune!
Hyacinths at Easter
And narcissus in a bowl
With white pebbles around them!
The March wind on Walnut Street Bridge
And the bells of Saint Marks,
And the bells of Holy Trinity,
And the bells of Saint Patricks—
Sound in the air
Floating over Rittenhouse Square!
The sun setting over the Locust Street gardens
And the starry night—beautiful in extreme!
Came then the fall from innocence
And slowly, imperceptibly,
I, We lost our world——

Long Ago

The bougainvillaea vine falls purple down the wall
  The sea grape tree stands tall and twisted—
Into the mind comes the song of the fountain splashing,
    ——and the sound of the sea
  Coming over the garden wall is forever—
When will memory not remember,
  And ears not hear
The shivering rustle of the palm trees in the wind?
  Is there a place distant enough
To drown the music of the mockingbird?
  I think there is not——
And that forever behind the eyes
  Will be the white walls and the tiled roof,
The sea grape tree and the fountain splashing—
  And the ears holding
The sound of the wind and the sea—
  And the eyes seeing through
    forever—forever—forever
To another time——

The Photograph

There's a photograph upon my wall
  Done by a master hand,
It's caught the timelessness of all,
  The sea, the ship, the land—
The ancient schooner's sails are full,
  The sea is riding free,
Bear Island Light, the rugged coast,
  Incomparable to see!

The Winter of Discontent

At Maximes they are playing
    the *Merry Widow*,
Outside it is raining,
  the rain hits the street
  like little wet stones—
The rain runs
  first black, then gold,
Under the street lamps—
  Shoes go by—
    and licorice black pumps move
    Under broadcloth trousers
  Splashed in crystal streaks—
    Emerald stiletto heels
    dance like grasshoppers
      through the rain
And the lady drops her flower—
  "Madame, Madame, votre fleur!"
Disdain sears him—there are many
    more flowers!
A blue-eyed boy sees the beautiful ankles
  Go through the door,
    And whistles—
The violins change to an accordion
  Pushing out notes in quick jerks,
And the dancers jig close in the hot room—
  The rain comes into the wineglass
Like tears—like tears!

Christmas—1962

Star-shingled night
    where followed
  their heart's way—
while the voices of the children
Holy Night
    sang out!
clear adolescent—
  unbeknowing of the rosewell—
  knowing the Magi,
    the Star,
      the Child—
clear, pure, the voices
    of the children—
untouched, unbeknowing
  of the rosewell
    coming after—
the permissions of maturity
  in the human world!

No Chipmunk

Today I saw no chipmunk,
No shadow at the door
No little anxious face that hoped
for flower seeds some more!

No tiny fleeting shadow,
No rustle in the grass
Not even a demanding chirp
Above me as I pass

From one house to another
On the well beaten way—
O chip, maybe the last I'll see
Of you, was yesterday!

So Chip, if in your tunnel
You lie in furry ball
There is no other animal
That I will miss at all—

And when you wake in springtime
O I hope that I'll be there
To see you show your little head
And sniff the soft spring air!

The Last Trout

He lay on his back
  In the ditch—
The sky looked blue and high—
  His head pounded;
"Is it my heart,
  Or the guns,
Or is it someone breathing
      beside me?"
  But he could not turn his head—
He felt a terrible wetness in his shirt,
Water—? No, not water, or was it?
  He rolled his eyes upward,
"That's a summer sky—" he thought,
"Like June at home—
  High and blue—fishin' weather!"
Suddenly he heard the stream running in his head—
"One more cast an' I'll git you, trout!"
  His eyes closed again—
"———Water—! I'm in deep water!
  Wadin' through deep water!
  ———O my Lord, my Almighty God—I'm a-comin'
  Through the deep water
  I'm a-comin——
With a fish for You—!"

To A Friend Who Died Too Soon

Too soon to leave!
  I wish you hadn't gone!
There was so much still to say,
  O, O —
I feel like the Chinese woman
  Rocking in her grief
Or the Indian woman
  chanting "ai ai"
In her bottomless sorrow—
  I think you know everything now,
    the unanswerable
      Is answered—
The metaphysical mysteries
  Melt into clarity—
The streams of Heaven run silver and gold
And we know now you will never grow old!
Your spirit fleet as an arrow will fly
For eternal life can never die—

Happening

It could have been,
    And was not—
And it was,
    And never took place—
And knowing this
    As one might in a crystal ball,
It filled all needs,
    The vein and the heart,
And the passionate soul!
    Only it never was—
But it happened!
    Green, green green memory,
Memory ever green!

The Seminoles

I remember the sun and the sand,
The heat, and the palms, and the flat land—
The hyacinth-choked canals, the long straight road,
The wild Everglades swamp where the heron strode—
The Great Blue heron, the flamingo, the crested egret,
The Tamiami Trail, the heat and the dust, and the sweat—
I can see in my mind's eye the Seminoles—
    I can see them yet,
Coming from afar off, coming from the right,
In their long canoes of cypress, heavy as night—
From the hammock behind them smoke rose in windless air,
They paddled very near us, we saw their black straight hair—
They wore many colors—reds, yellows, greens, and blues,
Ah, they looked magnificent in their long black canoes!
I remember the clear water, the saw grass, and three snakes
That slithered into the water where the reed stalk breaks,
The moccasin opened its white cotton mouth in fear
As it rippled through the water, "Get out of here!"
We yelled at the snake in panic—the Seminoles did not jeer,
Their silence was a knife of scorn, and I saw their hostile eyes
Appraising us with icy and contemptuous surprise—
How black, and straight, and thick their hair—like a cap!
And the look behind their eyes was a fierce, sullen slap
Of eternal, ancient rage—"Come into this Kingdom if you dare!
With your thin white skin, and your thin, fair hair!

Weak-brained that must wear a hat, weak-footed that must
        wear a boot,
You would die if you ate of the wild popple-root—
Our succulent raw fish would choke you!"—their eyes
       said this,
As they came so near us we heard the paddles hiss—
They went to the westward—ah, we could not follow!
We had no cypress dugout, long and hollow—
I remember snowy egrets rising in a cloud,
As they paddled slowly westward, remote, and dark, and
  proud—
But we were interlopers, we had trod on sacred ground,
With longing eyes we watched them, but they never
  looked
        around!

The Deer

Hoofs in mud,
    Ears back,
Long necks to water
    They drank—
A crow cawed—
    Flung water drops
Flashed in answer—
    And they fled!
Snorting—leaping—
    White tails flaring
"Beware! Beware!"

Cape Horn

We passed the Horn
    at daylight—
The seas slid under us
  Like mountains,
Because we were in the
    meeting place
  Of oceans—
One glimpse we had—
  That was all—
The great outer-most rock,
  The Horn!
A black fort guarding the Straits—
  Then fog like smoke—
And we saw no more—
  We were left
With the sliding stupendous sea,
    The salt wrack
Flowing behind us—
    And the voice
  Of the old man,
Roaring above the wind—
  "Grog for all hands, Mister,
We have made our Westing!"

The Storm

Black wind,
    Black day,
Black sea all around,
And we homeward bound!
The wind tearing at the ship
With a devil's grip,
Hanging to the yard
Was hard,
With the salt like a whip
To your lip,
And the wind
And the sail
And the sea,
A force
in Trinity!
Batter, and bluster and hiss!
Shall we ever get out of this!
Lads, shall we see once more
The green of our native shore?
We are swinging mighty high
Up here in the darkling sky—
We are still so far from land!
But Lord—we are in Thy hand!
Look now!—by the rolling mast,
The Evening Star at last!
And a streak of gold on the heaving breast
Of the sea that slides to the rainy east,
O Lord, we are in Thy hand!

The Kingdom of Heaven

Over moon-moss
  And through clover-valley
He entered into the Kingdom of Heaven,
"O long lost!" said the Angel Gabriel,
"Art thou glad to be here?
Or did'st thou love the world unbearably?"
And he answered, "I loved the world so much
That when the Lord called me
And I heard thy trumpet, Gabriel,
And knew my time had come,
Tears burnt me—
And though I answered
  As I knew I must,
I could not forbear listening
  For the last time
To the birds about my house—
  Could not forbear
To touch the bloodroot and anemone
  One long last time—
And O the pear tree standing by my door—
  Never——O nevermore
To see it blossoming!"
  Soft, soft were the eyes of the Angel Gabriel
"Did'st thou not cherish the Lord," he said,
"Faithfully through thy life?
Did'st thou not carry His shield
Through joy and pain?"

"O look before thee!
There is everything—

Thy house, thy birds and flowers—
Even thy pear tree
   Standing all in bloom!"—

So did he enter
   into the Kingdom of Heaven.

The Caught Fish

O carry me to water
  Where I can feel the sea,
Before I feel the dying
  Of too much air in me—!

Your silver trinket tempted,
  I bit deep on the hook
Brought swirling to the surface
  A chance that I mistook—!

O burly form above me,
  Your eyes are full of pride—
How can your nature triumph
  Because a fish had died?

He slips his hand beneath me
  Against all reason's rhyme,
Restoring me to ocean
  Just in the nick of time!

O Lord, Thy fish returneth
  To frolic in the sea!
Back to my natural living
  A creature made by Thee—

The Lost Island

I remember the Island
  Grey and still,
Long and rocky,
  Like the top of a hill—

The seabirds flew
  Round and in front,
Even not seen at all
  I heard their haunting call—

It echoed over the Island
  Wild and shrill,
And the sound of the sea
  Rolled over the Island's hill—

In summer, beguiling
  The Island lies
Like a great sea beast asleep
  To enraptured eyes—

In winter a different story,
  Rough waves beating in,
And the Island shows its grey strength
  Waiting for the winter to begin.

The Union Jack

High flies the flag of England,
  Taut stretched to the wind and true!
Saint George's cross streams onward
  Holding the red and blue—

This to the world no stranger,
  Flag of an island race,
Civilization's banner
  Full of glory and grace!

To him who in battle stranded,
  Raises his dying eyes
To glimpse the flag he fought for
  Painting the sunset skies,

O watch for the flag of England!
  As it streams in the wind's soft flow,
For who-so lives beneath it
  Is free to come and go.

Free to follow their pathway
  Whither or where it leads—
But wherever they rest at the ending,
  Tis English blood that bleeds—

They may speak in a different language,
  Or drive in a bullock cart,
They may have an adopted country,
  But England is in their heart—

O watch for the flag of England!
  Flag of an island race
Civilization's banner,
  Full of glory and grace!

Sonnet

Now looms the Cornish Coast—the voyage is done.
The cliffs of England stand in rocky might,
And the high Fate by Destiny begun
Leaps toward its purpose, as a meteorite
Blazes through Heaven to the earth's dark heart—
So with these lovers standing face to face
Locked in each others eyes, yet still apart,
By mystic passion held without embrace,
And drowned in rapture deep beyond compare.
This was a love to dare the depths of fire,
Assail the peaks of joy or wild despair,
Implacable in its profound desire.

The fateful hour is come—the die is cast—
Tristan picks up the cup and drinks at last.

Differences

O many kinds of loving
   Endow the human heart
Tempestuous or selfish,
   Too close or far apart

But there is one affection
   A very special kind
It meets with storm and shadow
   And to most faults is blind—

It weathers wind and weather,
   And turns the other cheek
And if you really need it,
   It's never hard to seek.

It wears no plumes of purple,
   It has no crown of gold,
In triumph and disaster
   Its banner high to hold!

You'll know it by the feeling
   Of love's supreme surmise—
And by the sudden tears that come
   And wash across your eyes,

Be not surprised by feeling
   And let it have its way,
For family affection
   Has got you in its sway!

La Strada

Black is the color of the day,
   And flags in the spiritual mind
      Are at half-mast—
Even though the wind blows on freedom,
   There is darkness here—
Money changes from hand to hand,
   And there is the sound of someone weeping—
Artichoke Head goes off with the Black Clown—
   How dark it is!
A cloud has gone over the sun—
   The black van of the motorcycle
Reduces into distance—
   And the round black eyes
      Look back,
      Look back,
      Look back—

If only her cloak had not been so thin and ragged
   Against the wind!

Sonnet to Keats

Let the cold earth come down upon the heart,
Let the dim worm dissever flesh from bone,
Let the rain fall, and let the sun impart
Its health to this corruption. Let the stone
Be now a pillow for that wondrous head
To rest vexation. Let the dear sleep come
At weary last. O be forever fled
From this pinched world that proved so poor a home
To your distracted being! Know that now
You cannot be forgotten where you are.
The laurel leaves already on your brow
Descend in green and holy avatar.
Know too this wide oblivion from strife
Becomes your Resurrection and your Life.

The Turtle

Oh patient turtle digging in the sand
Thy careful preparations for a birth—
Thy journey from the sea
To higher shore,
Thy hole, thy hiding place
For life to come,
Thy law and ours the same—all, all ordained
As that which ordains us—

Oh lowly, tired creature
So far—spent,
Thou canst but barely move
Thy heavy weight—
Thy work is done, thy destiny fulfilled—
There in the sand deep down
Thy treasure lies,
Secret, and round, and white,
The pearly eggs that were thine agony,
Holding the life to come—
Oh, now see thee
With flippered tenderness
Pat down their roof of sand to keep them safe!
And then thyself
Must struggle from the hole,
Scarce able now
To manage it—
Must turn thy clumsy self
Towards the sea,
And lumbering, lurching, swaying,
Make thy way
Across the sliding beach—
I know, I watched, oh breathless for thy sake,
And saw the tears fall heavy from thy lids!
I watched thee meet the ripple,

Saw thee go
Like Fate itself
Into the waiting sea—
In strength and pain—
Like very love itself
Unknowingly!

Night Club

This cross against my cross,
   And under well—
Below well bottom
   And secret in the earth,
Stirs pain—
   The looking through
Into the well remembered garden
   Whose gate is locked—
The high wall
   Over which the scent of flowers came,
Drifting through air—
   Not the garden, though like,—
Not the flowers,
   Nor the scent of them—
But a gate of iron,
   Inflexible—
By distance deceived
   By maturity removed—
     ——Yet there——

Maine

Pine trees and granite
Reaching into sea;
Mountains low-lying,
This is Maine to me.

Mud flats gold and gleaming
At the low tide,
Lonely outer islands
Where the great seas ride;

The southwest wind is hazy,
The northwest wind is clear,
The east wind has a cold blue light
That brings the islands near.

The south wind pushes in the fog
Grey-fingered like a ghost,
In clouds of mist it slowly comes
And swallows up the coast.

It slides up on the mountains
And veils their granite heads,
With watery weight it settles down
And slowly slowly spreads

In wide engulfment up the Sound,
Till shore and boat and pier
In outline blurred and dim become
Until they disappear.

Two Deer

Coming by Upper Hadlock in the dawn
Fog on the ground and stars thick overhead,
Straight in the glow of headlights saw we fawn
And doe beside him out of leafy bed—
Poised like two fairy creatures caught in light,
Startled to stillness, soft eyes all ablaze,
They stood transfixed upon the edge of flight
Motionless as a carving on a vase!
Swift to appear, like lightning did they go,
White tails a-bob, black noses snorting steam,
The leaping fawn behind the leaping doe
Like recollections of a vanished dream—
Into the woods they went, but left with me
The magic moment—and the memory!

Man

Tall, strong,
Like a song;
Great, bursting,
Hungering, thirsting;
Crying out
In a shout;
Looking far
To a star;
Digging down,
Splitting stone;
Shovelling sand
With tired hand;
Picking rock
Out of muck;
Building up
To the top;
Building high
To the sky.
Man, tough fibred,
Hard, untired;
Harried by both joy and pain,
By the diamond of his brain,
By Ambition's deadly fire,
By his own supreme desire,
Harried by a million things—
This is Man, and yet he clings
Like a limpet to this life,
Like a child he clings to wife;
Children also, boys and girls,
Are his ego, are his pearls;
To his home
Must he come;
To the end
This is friend;

His last breath
Drawn with death,
Calls aloud,
All his proud
Vigor fights
At this ending of his nights,
At this ending of his days,
At this parting of his ways.
Death is stronger,
Time is longer,
Close his eyes,
So he dies.

Achilles Heel

Wide-stretched to split fire
   The mark of the heart's burning—
The fatal thrust of the flung spear
   pierces the warm flesh to anguish—
      ——The blazing blood
takes into itself the tears—
      ——the sun flecks
   through the olive leaves
gold spots of dancing—
the wind brings the sound of the sea
   to the leaves' harp—
distilling through its fluttering sweet
      strings forever
   the dark passion of the wound
   the terrible slow grief——

Concerto

Dark room
  And moonlit sea through window
And three people staring at the sea
  While the *Grieg Concerto* played—
    Notes of music in the dark
      Falling like balm—falling like mercy
On the anguish—

Darkness
  Merciful too
  Wrapped around us
O protection of darkness
Hiding the red staining of the wound!

Below Surface

Holding to—
    and not holding to—
And the chute of tears between—
    Anguish of heart,
or anguish of imagination—
    and truth covered over
by waves of tenderness,
    only to appear
again—
    a sooner time—
a later time—!
    truth hard and rocky
pushing above
    the waters of tenderness
To tear the leaping body
    In the sea—

Where?

In dark streets turning,
Midnight oil run out,
And shadow meeting shadow on the stair,
Asking the question
"Where?"———
Listen alone—and to the heart alone
That answers, could one hear it—
"There!"

A Voice Speaks In Hades

"Crying out—more than weeping—
This is what we heard at Mithros—
And the great bronze hinges
Splitting and bursting from their sockets in the wall,
As the Doors of the City fell—
O never, never did we think they would!
The sound of their falling
Was louder than the winter sea
At Mitylene—
And the dust rushed out from beneath
In an evil cloud!
Chanting they came
And we heard the sound of their sandals
Slapping on the wood of the fallen doors as they entered
    our City—
We heard the quick hiss of the flung spears,
And the sudden terrible battering of the shields—
We fought, hand to hand,
Dying in hot blood before them,
But they were too much for us—
Like the sea, they filled our streets,
Sweeping all before them—
Not more purple the plumes of their helmets
Than their feet with our blood!
We heard only the terrible death shouts,
No weeping—
We were all, all of us, slain—"

Landing

    The leaning ships beat in
Against the strong and straining tide.
Over the harbor burns a thin
    Moon, and the wide
Insistent night hangs close. A sudden din
    Of seamen's voices—then
The creak of lowered sails, the loud
Rattle of rasping anchor chain—
    A vagrant cloud
Over the moon—and all is still again.

The House

There was a house
And its roof was red,
Spanish tiles from Spain!
A patio soft and green and cool,
And an old wellhead
With a mirrored pool,
And an emerald lizard
That came and went
Like a streak of color
That was not there,
Though it had been just beside your chair—
You sat in the garden and heard the train
Whistling its way up North again,
But not for me, you thought, not today—
Here is the place I wish to stay,
In this quiet house,
In this secret place,
Where the World outside
Cannot show its face—
Over the high white garden wall
I can see the palm trees green and tall,
I can hear the sound of the restless sea
Coming over the wall to me—
I can see the bougainvillea burn
Orange and purple—I can learn
Many things from the Mockingbird
Though we do not communicate by word—
And he is busy as he can be
In the sun-drenched, wild, old, sea-grape tree—
The flowers and I, we love the sun,
And we like to hear the fountain run—
But I remember the sound of a voice
That used to make my heart rejoice—
A voice that I will not hear again—

Can the garden hold my weight of pain?
Can the sea be still, can it take my tears
That fall in a length of fifty years?
Can the Mockingbird
Restore my heart?
Can I to the lizard
My grief impart?—
The bougainvillea's purple stain
Brings forth the blood of my heart again—
The house is there,
The enchanted place—
The patio with its fairy grace!
But the time is over—I cannot stay—
For the figure I loved has gone away.

Hurdy-Gurdy Monkey

You've got a little hat,
  And a little red coat—
And you dance on the tips of your toes!
You have anxious eyes
  And a tamborine,
And a blunted monkey nose—
  You dance to the music
  One, two, three,
Till the endless tune is done—
  And the children throw a penny
In your tamborine
  While you stand there in the sun—
Your owner gives a twitch of his hand
  And you leap
To his shoulder proud and high
  And I watch you go down
    the hill to the town
Your coat flaring out,
  And your hat like a crown,
You've forgotten you were ever
  A dancing clown,
Sweetness and bitterness
  Riding high,
A man and his Monkey
  Against the sky!

Street Corner

The rain falls on the house,
On the streetcorner,
On taxicabs,
On the autumn trees,
On people walking
Alone or together—
Alone may not be alone,
Or together together—
And loneliness a heady drink,
Or a fatal one—
And your cap is over the windmill
And all chips falling—
Or your cap is in the gutter
With you—
And the broken life—
And the falling house,
And the black rain
Raining in your black heart—

At the Cafe the lights are on
And the smell of meat and wine
Slides through the door
Into the night—into the street—
Into the rain—

The night darkens
And the rain blackens
In your black heart—
Hunch your shoulders against the rain—and memory—

The sword swallower in the Arcade
Wears a spangled dress,
Her hair is oiled and scented—
It glitters as she tilts her head back
To swallow the sword!

O watch with what ease—with what ease the blade goes
   down!
And at least you are out of the rain!
White round throat
Is there no bleeding from the blade?
O woman in the spangled dress,
Can you swallow the sword when you are alone—
When there is no audience—?
No applause—?
In the room you go to is there warmth?
Someone waiting—or waiting for—
Or a cat—or a dog—
Or a creature of any kind
For comfort?
—Or do you too
Hunch your shoulders against the rain,
Feeling its black tears
Scald across your heart—!

The Window
Saint Mary's by the Sea
for ACY and CY

Blue for truth
  Where honor stood,
Red for courage,
  Gold for good;
Burning green
  For all the years,
Purple for the
  Hidden tears;
Amber for
  the last content
Wrested from
  Relinquishment!

The Song
to A.C.Y.

How unerringly you played your life
Like a bow string
    always true!
O the fidelity of the music,
Whether gay or sad!
The notes you made sounded
    in other lives
    their sweetness
    or their darkness—
You rang like a song long after
In the memory under and through,
As if a person would say,
"O what is that long lost music?"
And then remember it was you!

Ships

Blue sea flowing between me and the shore,
I will watch at the beginning of evening the shadowed
Ships as before,
Coming between me and the land, one, two, three, four;
Dreaming they sail over the ocean floor,
In from the ends of the earth with their golden store,
As before.

The Pine Tree

Sweeter than honey,
  Smoother than flax,
Ripe to the flung hand,
  Soft to the axe—

So fell the big tree,
  Large and as tall
As giants in stories,
  Taller than all!

Sharp was its scent
  As it fell on the morning,
Strong with its balsam
  It lay felled, adorning

The dark earth around it
  With beautiful length,
Ah, pity the pine tree
  Cut down in its strength!

For Anna-Sophia
How Brave You Were!

I remember the sled and the snow
   As we went down together—
Because you were the eldest
   You steered
And I stuck on behind,
   Clutching your body and your legs—
The snow had an icing on top
   So we went very fast,
Suddenly the icing broke through
   And we stopped!
I saw your head in its little winter hat
   Go down——
You did not move
   And suddenly I saw the snow
Turning red under your face!
   A kind man came running
And picked you up,
   I followed with the other children,
They laid you on the billiard table
   Flat—
And gave you hot cocoa—
   You never spoke and never cried,
A doctor came,
   "She has broken her nose" he said
You were in great pain
   O, I have never forgotten!

We went home then
   In the carriage
I could still see the blood on the snow
   As I see it now—
And still you did not cry——
   How brave you were!

The Orchard

When you asked I could not answer,
  But I can answer you now—
I can tell you about the apple smell,
And how the field mice nibbled at the
      sweet roots
    of the old trees!
How the meadow ran down
    to the stream,
How we built up the broken fence
And pruned the trees neglected
    for so long—
We borrowed a press and made cider
    in the autumn,
  The raw juice
    Tasted like sweet wine,
And we knew we had saved the orchard
    from the past!
I could not talk of it
  When you asked me,
Because in the end
  We lost it all—
And I could not bear to remember
  For the tears!

For Anna-Sophia
Do You Remember?

You said you knew all the time
But did you—
Did you know when the smell of
   roasting chestnuts came through the window,
How the library vanished,
And the Square came into view—
The old Square where the children skated
And where the young man in the
   black velour hat
Walked across in the morning!
Did you know about the hurdy-gurdy,
And the knife grinder,
His bells and his voice
Coming up through the window
From the life of the street outside?
And later the sunset came across the gardens
From Holy Trinity,
Now that was such a very long time ago!

Revolution

Counter blood current to counter heart
   storm to stillness
Becoming storm to storm
   Becoming pitted against
Becoming locked agonizingly
   Until death for one
And Flag flies
   Over snow-hill
Dark wood
   Wheat plain
Field, fence, farmhouse,
   Black-iced creek—
Flag made of wounds—
   Snow—suffering
Flag made of Freedom!

My Dog

My dog had melting eyes
  Clear and brown,
A trusting forehead
  That could not frown—
A sturdy paw,
  And a tail that told
Whether the heart was
  Warm or cold—
Ready for silence,
  Ready for talk,
Always ready
  To share a walk—
Where is my dog,
  O where is she?
Who always wanted to walk with me—
  Can she hear my voice,
Can she know my grief,
  Can she feel my tears
Through the rusting leaf?
  O Lord, let my Dog
Achieve her place
  In Thy Heavenly Meadows
Beneath Thy Grace—
This is my prayer O Lord
That she
  Rest in Thy love in her dog's degree—

The Christmas Tree

The Christmas tree stands in the corner
   Wearing its stars and bells,
Holding proudly the silver Angel on its head,
Stretching its green arms wide
   For the gold glass swans,
For the glittering magic birds,
   For the sharp emerald horns,
And the crackling ruby rope
   Of fluted tinsel winding through and about
      Up to the Angel!
The Christmas Tree is *alive!*
   It has forgotten, for the moment,
      The agony of the axe,
And the long hours afterwards
   When it lay numb and almost lifeless,
      Waiting to be chosen—
But now——
   Loving hands have carried it home,
   Have gently unfolded the stricken branches,
They have hung it from tip to toe with
      gold and silver,
   And it holds the Christmas Angel on
      its head!
   The Christmas tree stands,
Trembling a little in its beauty—
   It waits for the supreme moment
      Of Christmas,
When the eyes of the children shall behold it
   With rapture and wonder—
      It stands proudly in the darkened room,
      Waiting, waiting!

It has almost forgotten the Forest——
      But not quite!